Many thanks to . . .

My husband Gil for his ongoing support and
inspiration,

My daughters Daphna and Dahlia for helping
me see Israel from a child's point of view,

My parents Sara and Nissim who taught me to
love Israel from an early age,

Sigalit Davis, Hebrew Language Instructor and
my colleague and friend at Hebrew College, for
her help with the Hebrew in this book   — R.R.

Text and photos copyright © 2015 by Rachel Raz
Photos of cow and street signs by Daphna Raz. Photo of
prayer book by Dahlia Raz.

KAR-BEN PUBLISHING
An imprint of Lerner Publishing Group, Inc.
241 First Avenue North
Minneapolis, MN 55401 USA
1-800-4-KARBEN

Website address: www.karben.com

Main body text set in Kidprint MT Std.
Typeface provided by Monotype Typography.

Library of Congress Cataloging-in-Publication Data

Raz, Rachel, author, photographer.
    The colors of Israel / by Rachel Raz ; photos by
Rachel Raz.
       pages   cm.
    ISBN: 978–1–4677–5539–9 (lib. bdg. : alk. paper))
    1. Colors—Juvenile literature. 2. Hebrew language—
Dictionaries—English—Juvenile literature. 3. Colors,
Words for—Juvenile literature. 4. Signs and symbols—
Juvenile literature. 5. Israel—Juvenile literature. I. Title.
QC495.5.R39   2015
956.94—dc23   2014029043

Manufactured in China
2-36801-17693-8/4/2022

0423/B0808/A2

The Colors of Israel

PHOTOGRAPHS AND TEXT BY RACHEL RAZ

KAR-BEN
PUBLISHING

A double-decker train in Akko

Red

A-dom • אָדוֹם

Stoplight

Israeli mail van

Ka-tom • כָּתֹם
Orange

Umbrellas on the
Tel Aviv beach

Fresh juice at the Jaffa market

Tree blossoms
in the city of
Giv'atayim

Yellow

Tza-hov • צָהוֹב

At the bus station

The cable car
at Rosh Hanikra

Green

Ya-rok • יָרוֹק

Cactus
(Sabra)

Bikes for rent in Tel Aviv

A recycling bin

Blue
Ka-chol • כָּחֹל

The Israeli flag

The Haas Promenade in Jerusalem

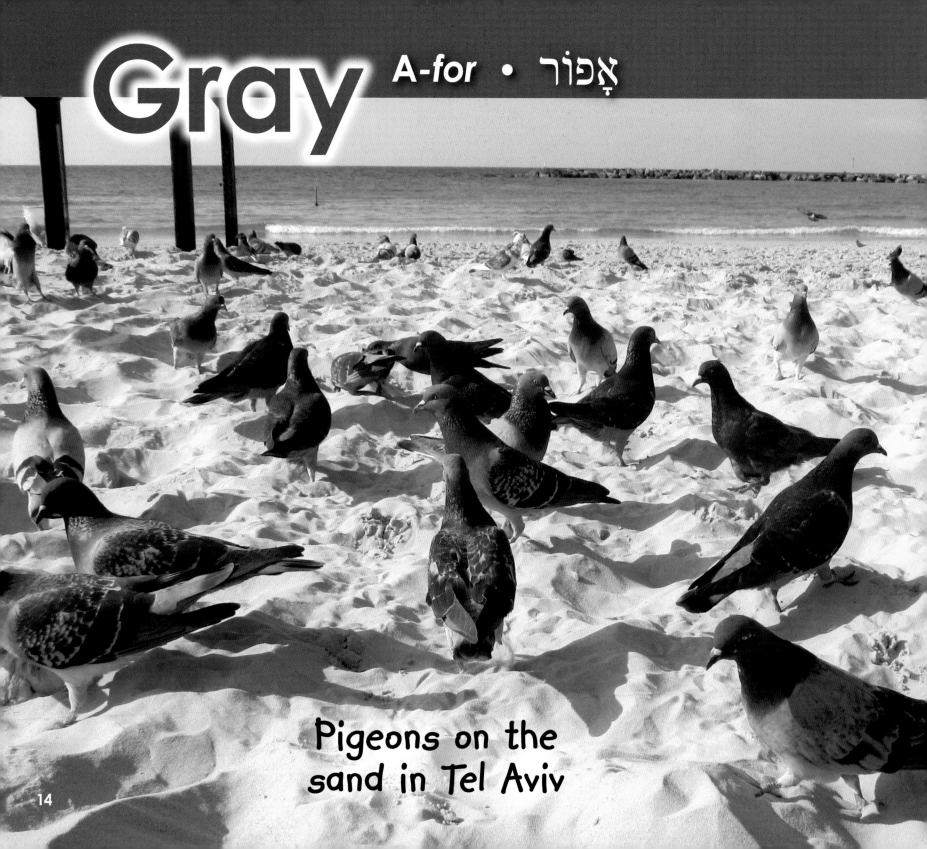

Gray

A-for • אָפֹר

Pigeons on the
sand in Tel Aviv

Bench and trash can in Jerusalem

Fresh challah
at the market

Brown

Choom • חוּם

A cow in the
Golan Heights

Sufganiot (jelly
doughnuts) at
the market

black

Black flags at the beach
mean "be careful"

דרך השלום

طريق هشالوم

DEREKH HASHALOM

Hebrew, English, and Arabic signs

White

La-van • לָבָן

Montefiore
Windmill in
Jerusalem

Prayer book at the
Western Wall

The Shrine of the Book,
home to the Dead Sea Scrolls

Pink

Beautiful cyclamens

Stamps of Israel for
mailing letters

Sculpture at the
Ein Hod Artists Village